What's the Difference?

Cheryl Jakab

Momentum
What's the Difference?

First published in Great Britain in 1998 by

Folens Publishers
Albert House
Apex Business Centre
Boscombe Road
Dunstable
Beds LU5 4RL

© 1998 Momentum developed by Barrie Publishing Pty Limited

89 High St, Kew, Vic 3101, Australia

Reprinted 1999

British Library Cataloguing in Publication Data.
A Catalogue record for this book is available from the British Library

ISBN 1 86202 422 7

Designed by Pauline McClenahan
Printed in Singapore by PH Productions Pte Ltd   .

Every effort has been made to contact the owners of the photographs in this book. Where this has not been possible, we invite the owners of the copyright to notify the publishers.

A.N.T. Photo Library/Nigel Dennis p. 14; A.N.T. Photo Library/Frank Park p. 14; A.N.T. Photo Library/David Paton p. 11; A.N.T. Photo Library/Ron & Valerie Taylor p. 14; A.N.T. Photo Library/Dave Watts p. 13; Horizon Photo Library pp. 9, 10, 17, 20, 21, 22; International Photographic Library cover, pp. 4, 5, 6, 7, 8, 9, 10, 12, 15, 16, 18, 22; B. Silkstone pp. 6, 8, 19, 22; Ken Stepnell pp. 15, 18; Bill Thomas p. 11.

Contents

What Is That?

Could you tell the difference between a lion and a tiger when you were very young? Do you know which is which when you look at these animals now? Could you tell someone else what the differences are?

Do you know that lions and tigers are both members of the cat family? They are mammals in the group called felines. All the things they have in common make them both felines. The differences between them make one a lion and the other a tiger.

Have you ever wondered what the difference is between a butterfly and a moth?

What is the difference between a monkey and an ape?

Can you look at a turtle and know that it is a turtle, not a tortoise? How would you tell the difference?

This book is about how we tell the difference between animals that are very much alike.

What's the Difference Between a Butterfly and a Moth?

Look carefully at the pictures.

What do you think might be some differences between a butterfly and a moth?

Butterflies and moths both belong to the same group of insects. One way to tell them apart is to look at their wings when they land.

Butterflies usually hold their wings up when they land. Moths do not usually do this. Their wings usually lie flat. But this is not a sure test.

The easiest way to tell a moth from a
butterfly is to study their antennae.

The antennae of a butterfly are usually
shaped like clubs. The antennae of a moth
usually look feathery.

There is another way to tell these insects
apart. Butterflies are usually active in daylight.
Moths are usually active after dark.

So, which of these are butterflies and which are moths?

What's the Difference Between a Turtle and a Tortoise?

Look carefully at the pictures.

What do you think might be some differences between a turtle and a tortoise?

Turtles and tortoises are both reptiles. Both have hard shells.

Turtles usually live in water. They have webbed feet or flippers for swimming. Turtles eat both plants and animals.

Tortoises are land-living turtles.

Most tortoises have high, rounded shells.
They have strong <u>limbs</u> for walking on land.
Their front legs are covered with hard scales.
Tortoises eat only plants.

So, which of these are turtles and which are tortoises?

What's the Difference Between a Frog and a Toad?

Look carefully at the pictures.
What do you think might be some differences between a frog and a toad?

Frogs and toads are both amphibians. One way to tell frogs from toads is that most adult frogs live in or near water. Most adult toads live on land.

The main feature that distinguishes frogs from toads is that toads tend to have drier, lumpier skins than frogs. Toads also have shorter and less powerful back legs than most frogs.

So, which of these are frogs and which are toads?

What's the Difference Between an Ape and a Monkey?

Look carefully at the pictures. What do you think might be some differences between an ape and a monkey?

Monkeys and apes are both primates. There is one main difference between a monkey and an ape. Most monkeys have tails, but apes do not. Some monkeys can use their tails like an extra arm. They use their tails to hold things or to hang in trees. These kinds of tails are called prehensile.

Apes vary
greatly in size,
from the gibbon
to the gorilla.

21

So, which of these are monkeys and which are apes?

Can you think of any other animals that are similar, but different? Perhaps you can find out what is the difference between a porpoise and a dolphin!

Glossary

amphibian an animal that lives part of its life in water and part on land

antennae a pair of moveable sensing 'feelers' on the head of some creatures

feathery soft, or looking like feathers

mammals warm-blooded animals that feed their young milk

prehensile able to grasp things by wrapping around them

primates the group of mammals that includes monkeys and apes; they usually have flexible hands with five fingers and flexible feet with five toes

Index